SUDDEN ANTHEM

SUDDEN ANTHEM

~~MATTHEW GUENETTE~~

[signature]

Holms—

Thank you for supporting the world! To ISU, & all things Masters!

— *[signature]*

Dream Horse Press
California

Library of Congress Cataloging-in-Publication Data:

Guenette, Matthew
        Sudden Anthem
                p.   cm

                ISBN 978-0-9777182-4-5
                1. Poetry

10 9 8 7 6 5 4 3 2 1

First Edition

Cover: "Wake Up Call" by Lynne Taetzsch,
        http://www.artbylt.com

Contents

SUDDEN ANTHEM

The Happening

We raced to the stores for ridiculous effects:
sombreros and clove cigarettes.
                Bought the extra-special toothpaste,

whitened our smiles
        like Scandinavian film queens
                with vodka in our veins. We jogged

the esplanade shins positively athrob
like the bedcovers in a Niagara Falls motel.
                Ve scooped for ze hundrezth time

ze kat box, grilled for ze hundrezth time
        ze grilled-cheese, read for ze hundrezth time
                ze book on vinning chess,

if only we could beat schizophrenic Wes
hanging around the corner's neck
like a sticky, daily special.

He Swiss-knifed us
        with the bishop's fianchetto,
                Budapested our ass with Hungarian Defense.

Oh Lord there was so much to forget: brain-
            roots for quadratic equations, a freight train
                of reasons for the failures

in our hearts, the definition of *gossamer* looked up
        a dozen times like a baby galaxy
stashed beneath a bed. Treading

this murky reservoir type water,
        this middle-America-in-debt-to-the-penny-water,
this need-to-skip-the-Midwest-pronto-water.

We kissed the nanosecond's
        beaded flash-lamp for luck and needed sherpas
to navigate our fucked-up ideas. Forget death.

What crept was the snake oil
of credit cards and bills, the United States
of Shopping Malls, dentists with their tyranny

of honorable intent, the sharp objects polished and glossed,
        the maddening suction and floss.
                We were half platypus half coelacanth, half

trapped like the middle chapters
        of *The Brothers Karamazov*.
                Along the razor's edge, a constant happening

happening on the horizon of our thoughts,
        before the afterbirth's ruptured membrane, beyond the
funeral's
                pre-Cambrian blues, looped toward forever

like *I Love Lucy* and nothing could escape it;
the soul's casino of shadows,
                its accountants metaphysical

who half-baked the books
        with a bottomless shoebox of miss-managed receipts.
                We wanted to slide our hands

up time's too-tight
        glitter skirt, wished desire's pierced cherry
tongue in our mouth.

Just one more game
        with schizophrenic Wes, who argued with himself
                like a theory, who disappeared

down the alley after every few moves
            but always returned wearing
completely different shoes.

Hush of Something Endless

One of those parties where I was the stranger,
the rest with celebrity faces
from dreams. Burt Reynolds mixing dirty
martinis. Ron Jeremy with his chubby
fingers in fondue. A barefoot
Madonna dancing under crimson lights,
breasts and hips red shivers with each turn.
I watched the city open its palm
of glitter, my thoughts glued
in unmaking. But a stone-rhined Dolly Parton
kept bringing more and more bottles of wine.
Pretty soon I was terrifically drunk,
tripping from room to room like one
of Faulkner's minor fools, telling ridiculous
lies to anyone who would listen.
I'm an ex-con, I said. *I hot-wired*
cars in the Pittsburgh of my youth.
To the woman who whispered her bed
in my ear: *I'm an orphan, stolen*
by gypsies from my native Ukraine. Spoke
without regret, stuck in the sap
of twenty-something and alone, my first night
in a new city minus friends
or sensible shoes. When the hostess was fed up
with my shit she showed me the door.
Sleep it off on the lawn.   A good idea.
As I stretched out in the cool,
my mind slid down its blue rail of otherness
that makes you a stranger even
to yourself. A cigarette flared in the dark,
hush of a woman's voice—*Hey*—bored
as late-night TV. *Tell me all about you.*
I pressed my hands to the grass to keep from
spinning away. *My name's Vince*, I said.
Where should I begin?

Problems of Transcendence

Not so much the moment you, focus
and lift—abuzz, ignoring everything
—save the falling back to earth. The evening
divides (in two) couplets.
Sizzle steak. Wasp's sting. Teaching us a lesson
—but the hell with that. —Everything has
a life of its own, even the forks.
Especially the forks. Our troubled labor
towards death. This goes
without saying but then
comes the fireflies doing what they do. The "I"
lifted —from another like a purse. Someone
—with crows
in their thoughts. The (drum roll) pre-seeding X then
1.) Night screws up the order like a dippy
waitress. 2.) Night-cracked finger bone.
3.) And look how helpless we are; that's one message.
Another is *huh?* and *what?* Some important
things we do without ever opening
 our eyes. You and I like stars before
constellations, the consequences
and benefits, etc. —Not in the ship's hold
starving (within) the 17th century.
Not some pope lo-o-oming, on the corner
some old man warning the final judgment.
The bridge: gone drinking. Usually
there's a woman involved, or so it has been
with me. Seismograph and sieve: even the "dream"
has its own -isms, its truck stops and punch
lines, we in the midst of its joke.

Hover

I was happy in those days
pirating my way
across storm-tossed rugs

sling-shooting wooden slugs
at the seven-seas
of cats that roamed

our home like restless ghosts.
I gagged my brother
Marty Farty and strapped him

to the mast: an arrow
with mop-haired aim,
emergency ladyfingers

stored in the hold, check.
Before eating the crayons
I wrote letters to my mother

who kept a widow's watch
in a far-away kitchen
waiting for the last

good man to appear:
a nebula's cherry
light from deep space.

Her sadness was bigger
than Sunday.
She loved us like only

a schizophrenic could
and cooked us BLTs.
Dear mom, I would write.

Ur a wicked pretty lady.
Please send more BLTs.
P.S. I told Marty Farty

he came from your Butt.
At night by flashlight,
the mystified oracle

I studied my list
of suspicious relatives:
Crazy Legs and Ava Peron

Grandpa the Place Kicker,
cousin Stretch McGretchen
flame-throwing

in Hell's Kitchen.
The birth smell
of lilacs and mud, the death smell

of giant ball bearings
rolling toward us
from the corners of dreams.

I wanted to surf time
on quantum waves,
wanted to gun down bad guys

and *be* the bad guys,
spinning on my head
like an Indian cyclone.

Once I lived beneath a table.
Once I lived in near-dark
like light below the horizon.

Once I lived like a sap-sucker
in the trees.
The names I tattooed in the bark

filled with sugary blood.

Li Poem

From his motel room on the harbor
Li Po enjoys the sun as it sets
on the last days of the fiscal year.
Soon executives will storm the square

wheeling one another in office chairs
decorating the magnolias
with toilet paper and photocopies
of Cathy's ass from accounting.

Li Po stirs the martini in his thoughts.
His father's words float up
from the one and only time they ever

met: beware smiling men
in business suits, especially if
they're cheering for something you've done.

Seven Busboy Propositions

I. The Problem of Being

surrenders to sweeping dirty forks spoons
knives paper plates into plastic bags
wipe the table down with a rag
use lemon where butter congeals
to yellow snot your tips wadded up
in your pocket wandering
stoned through the pre-dawn fog
with the knowledge you must
rise again in a few hours. Until then...

II. (The Assignment

drive through the drive thru
in reverse; put "everything"
you "say" in "quotes" above your "head";
ask customers how they feel
about the barometric pressure;
stand on a corner with a "paint me" sign
around your neck; eat a deep fried Twinkie;
interview a tin wreath; wear a tutu
to the rally; go roller derby style;
choose a lake to rule over you,
watch the light across its water;
if not a lake then a lover; if not a lover
then your laughter, a stranger with
opinions on the barometric pressure)

III. Meat Doily

Nietzsche with a mullet...

IV. The Ghost of Me

It already exists. It hurts me
we've not spoken yet, the misunderstandings
between us curious and neglected
like a jar of pickled pigs feet. My ghost should have
serious questions for me
like, *who do you think you are?* Or, *what the fuck?*
In return I would ask
what he remembers from the everything forgotten
so we might finally get on haunting
one another's confessions...

V. If: The Chaos

in a seafood restaurant bathroom stall
where a bag (it seems) of turds has exploded
the monastic turd disappeared
without a trace before the flush, the bank-
clerkly turd, the inexplicable turd
in a busy, well-lit
lobby, turds in which the busboy's diet
is clearly discerned, the doubtful turd
the turd modulating, the turd that says
thou hast, that engraves, sopranos, periscopes
(stood presumably on its end by its author)

rising improbably from
the public toilet, Hotel Turds
turds that prefigure a prison break, turds
that when we read into them read back into us
a quality they share with so many gods...

●●●●

VI. Lyric
More than once my 5th grade teacher
Mrs. Godshall called me
a "distraction." I remember being ashamed.
I started calling her Mrs. Hogballs
behind her back, then one fine summer night
egged her house into the sea...

●●●●

VII. If
luminous balloons snagged in the trees
like lassoed moons, a man wearing
a helmet with antlers affixed
wanders the parking lot
carrying an oar, nothing can be said,
with certainty, in the picnic area couples
tango in the rain, the gathering darkness
takes its chances, adjusting the scenes
accordingly...

Murphy's Law

-for Steve Forrester

Freya, our stoner goddess of hippy-chicks,
chain-smoked & flirted shamelessly
with the Half-Pint who kept

lining up free shots like a man
without a prayer. The Jersey City Rabbi
ordered fifths & sixths

while Persephone the Leather Queen
rocked her hips against the pinball machine
tilting hearts up & down the bar.

Even *Ring of Fire*
lit up the jukebox & then after that
Thin Lizzy's *The Boys are Back*.

An old drunk in the corner
shouted through his tobacco
stained beard. *You can all*

kiss my golden codger!
Outside it was April, light snow falling.
Inside, our Manassas Mauler

strapped on his paper
Dr. Zaius hat & offered to read palms.
We found the notebook under the pool table

propping up the shortest leg:
skip to the page where it says,
Elvis and Achilles, those fuckers could sing.

It should interest you to know
your name was also there, forcefully written
& several times in a row.

Remember to Watch!

The billboard's red commercial
looms a rotund deliveryman—
Doug Heffernan—

in fully fueled sitcom mode.
Watch *The King of Queens*—
incongruous rising

its shadow shadows
a stand of trees
a scatter of trailers

on an otherwise inconspicuous
drive (text, distortion)
it imagines motorists

crashing for a better look.
Somewhere some money
composes an index

of traffic-hazarding sound bites
as thought a la
Cheney & Bush.

The billboard is a systematic
deranging
distraction in its demanded form.

The poem tries to tell you this
as a thing not pressed
flat before your eyes.

Secret Life of the Coin-Operated Laundromat Owner

The lone cafe in Kentuckiana
not dedicated to our Savior Jesus Christ
as decorating motif,
but I had issues with the representational art.
The paintings were ripped off
from Balthus—
knee-high bobby socks, women stroking
cats, pianos vibrating like chakras neaby—
minus the menacing
sexual allusion. What good is that?
Sometimes I was the orchid's sparkplug.
Lots of my ideas
sprang from comic books.
I had x-ray vision wishes and flew around
in a jockstrap: red, white and blue.
One night I dreamt the strength
of Neptune's hammer.
I hovered like a bee
just inches above the sun, the whole congregation
withholding medicine
and water. Therapists said
it was chemical, that I lived in an age
of excessive excess when really
small potatoes and a smile
were all I needed.
As heavenly bodies go,
the barista was completely Copernican.
Spaghetti strap halter, hip-hugger
jeans, funky flip-flops, toenails decorated
Demolition Red.
Sweetheart, I thought, *I hate it when you leave,*
but I love to watch you go.
I heard Willie Nelson said that, and maybe
Hermes too.

I wanted to say something similar without
getting slapped or beer tossed in my face.
I foraged like a refugee
for durable solutions. I looked like a preacher
for something to blame: the 12th century,
NAFTA, pneumatically transported
germs in the crops.
The police scanners squawked
their tricky business like a bruised fist
for a heart. I thought
annihilate was too sentimental.
I thought if I held my ground like a claw-footed
tub, my iron sides would be filled
in one even flow.

Vortex: The Super-Sized Supermarket

For more than once
I've been elbowed in the ribs, made to ask

where are the q-tips? Where the re-fried beans?
For I've wandered cheese aisles so long

they had storm drains,
seen rows of frozen pizzas

vanish like pins on the horizon.
And when you catch yourself

humming something as vanilla
as Billy Joel's *In the Middle of the Night*

what's left but to set your head on fire?
Into what are we being undone,

receding from ourselves
like ice defrosts into mist? For one more

magazine charting the celebrity progress
of a partying heiress

rotting like a fish.
For one more mug shot of Tom Cruise

who looks just fucking crazy, his face
a hijacked car, his eyes headlights

bearing down a dark ravine.
For the endless packaging and meat shining

like the opposite of grace. For the barcode
rising hot on the back of my neck,

the dream of a lover's teeth
sunk into flesh. For the checkout line,

the teenager blithely
chewing gum who asks *paper or plastic?*—

these false dichotomies we pretend to
pretending to us in a discourse

of freezing and thawing,
cleaning and pre-heating—paper or plastic?

For that I say *dealer's choice*, and am met almost
always with suspicious stares.

Cauldron

The precinct had us voting at Georgia
O'Keeffe Middle School. The playground: a thing
of imaginings and easels, kids practicing
kissing the exquisite
with their messy *Jack in the Pulpits*. Over the intercom,
a secretary's white ribbon voice
announced Joey so-and-so was voted *Best at Selected
Perception*, Sarah so-and-so *Most Likely
to Wash in Oblivion*. When they asked me
to verify my address, I messed up,
said not "151 Rutledge" but "fur burger, hot dog style,"
a dirty dare my wife learned
from sons of Republicans at Impressionism
Junior High. She sings it sometimes
in the tub, in the moon's
calculated light, where naked she paints watercolors
of scarves, capturing the creepy
implications of what flowers in the intermittence...
I eyed my fellow citizens
marching toward the ballot box
like stony verbs. How would the limnologist with the red
mohawk vote? The guy with his fingers
in his mouth? The guy
with no arms?

Fracture Poem

When the fat guy gets hit by a bus
not once but twice he'll dress
like a Franciscan monk
forever after
and blame the government
for the new condos downtown.
The lipstick-lesbian
epileptic twenty-something
with Tourettes screams
"fuck it" at the bus stop
then composes an ode
as she seizures.
Her philosopher roommate
gets his bread from a soup kitchen
because he thinks paying for it
is too bourgeoisie
just like pronouncing your 'r's
is too bourgeoisie
or having parents
or buying a bungalow unless
the bungalow is in a neighborhood
where a bunch of cops
and firefighters live
and nobody pronounces their 'r's
or has parents.
A few blocks away the limnologist
falls in love with a chemist
the solipsist somnambulist
names her cat Rhoda
a man without a job figures out
a way to blow paint
through a straw
so the head he's drawing
looks like it exploded.

He has this pain
deep in his spiral galaxy.
When he concentrates real hard
he fixes himself
in the center of its landscape
which is a lifescape and orders
within the small parameter
some of the whatnot
around him so for a few
seconds it's not static anymore
it's a kind of music
the others can move to
a body held above.

I. Abstract Sex Positions

The Salacious Fitzpatrick
    Def-Con Fricassee
        The Stovepiped Bolshevik
            The Structuralist Controversy

The 2nd String Catcher
    Sweet & Sour Cha-Cha
        The Molly Thatcher
            The Oblivion Ha-Ha

Velvet Tourniquet
    The Humming Swede
        The American Parking Lot
            Confederates & Yankees

II. Other Items from Occam's Bathroom

Occam's toothpaste
    Occam's curlers
        Occam's acetaminophen

Occam's enema
    Occam's lube
        Occam's emergency ephedrine

Etymology

In New Hampshire where they call me *Gumby* or *Chigger* they'll never forget my shaved head, the orange goatee corkscrewing from my chin, the *Live Free or Die* tattooed across my face. They ache for me, my 3 or 4 friends, they tolerate my piracy and secret leftist military aide. Honorary member of the Harlem Globetrotters. The one who made *pants* a dirty word. Everybody laughed when I asked the regime for sixteen million, now I have this submarine and a truly magic 8-ball. I shake it, chance smiles and says, "All signs point to yes." In New Hampshire, they revel in my ideas. At dusk when the streetlights flicker like drunk stars, I sense the universe cooling in its mystery. I'm able to describe perfectly its tendrils that reach deep into the nothing that binds us.

Brief History of the Home Gym

Artifacts discovered in Babylonia
dating back to fourth century B.C.
suggest ideas of the first home gyms,
mechanisms that would boost metabolism
and predict orbits of planets and stars.
Gears on this earliest home gym
often jammed, as did the automatic looms
and levers, pretty much the problem
of home gyms for the next 2000 years
until Charles Atlas the Nascent, from Secaucus, NJ,
conceived of a home gym dubbed
The Difference Engine, a massive steam-powered
"conditional operator" shaped
like a saddled camel. He assembled this gym
over the course of 20 years.
Many ruptured triceps later, thin-shouldered
Federalists quit funding the deal. A century passed
before Konrad Von Trapezoid, German engineer
and would-be runway model, fashioned the first
general purpose home gym
to pioneer binary math and Boolean logic
in the abdominal muscle-crunch. In 1943, Colossus,
a British home gym prototype, was employed
to assist bodybuilders attain perfect homeostasis
while code breaking Fascist cryptograms.
Building on the colossal success of Colossus, ENIK,
the Electro Nitro Integrator Kartsonis,
was developed by ballistics firms
to promote fat loss and muscle tone
while firing artillery rounds at Foo Fighters
over Roswell, N.M. Like most home gyms of the day,
ENIK was the size of a fall-out shelter.
In the 50s J. Bell Laboratories assembled
the first transistor home gym, a biomechanically-

correct 8-by-11-foot fitness widget
that revolutionized smoothness, durability,
and introduced postal codes to Ottawa, Ontario.
Advances were made, costs for typical home gyms
fell to under $20,000. In the early 70s
Stuttering Flemish tribal chief
"Not Willing to Fornicate" began the Palo-
Latissimus Research Center
where the mission was, "to explore architectural
secrets to leaner, kick-ass bods."
Later during the Gulf Wars, radical handbills
dropped from black helicopters advertised 8-Mhz,
32-bit Motorola, Party Like It's 1999-Thousand
Home Gym Hard-Gainers with built-in
interactive battle maps, creatine myoplex stackers,
and a system of traffic signals
that encouraged fizzing sounds due to compressed
air bubbles popping in the polar ice.
These home gyms, nicknamed Donald
or Dickey, sold like smart bombs at the speed
of 12,000 per month. We predict home gym sales
will soon exceed one trillion dollars a day,
that a home gym will sit in the temple of every
American soul like bunker busting tension rods.
Fat will disintegrate like receipts in the laundry.
There will be no turning back.

Homeric

The slow one labeling boxes
was Virgil. That made the other jokers

I worked the line with
Homer and Ovid, part-time

cons who jibber-jabbered
like flyweights at the weigh-in.

Hey toilet face, get flushed. The Yankees
can suck my Beantown dick.

They punched in half-sauced
like fried eggs

hissing from the griddle
of the night before, 50 bucks lost

at the track, the old ball and chain
bitch-slapped good.

Picture an ass
three axe-handles wide.

That's my old lady. She's got a shitlist
half a mile long. We lived

like ridiculous cartoons,
with cannonballs

about to smash in our heads.
On smoke break

Homer peeled off his shirt
To show us his new tattoos.

They looked like zippers
across his wiry chest. I wondered

could we open him up,
stuff a new soul in there.

He was in my face flexing
like a four letter word.

Whatcha think Low Dog?
The ink swelled

like a bellow. The other guy, Ovid,
leaned against the bricks

with a mouth full of smoke. That left
just Virgil and me to answer,

Virgil who smiled his hot-water smile
and never said a word.

Amongst the Moon

A fist fight is like an orange peel but what came first,
Li Po challenges the mountain. Summer in the heartland.
A field. A bonfire. Li Po and the mountain
have been playing friendly drinking games all day
trying to get at the meaning of life, but now it's dusk
and the mountain is drunk and surly. In the Bible,
the mountain says, evening and morning were the fourth day,
and God said bring forth abundantly the fist fight.
Li Po does a shot. Yet in the *Origin of Species*,
he counters, Darwin says both the fist fight and orange peel
evolved simultaneously from a 24-hour diner.
The mountain rips of its t-shirt and gets in Li Po's face.
Time flows in the direction of unbecoming.
Some girls are laughing out in the woods. A fist fight
can't be born without an orange peel,
the mountain says, poking a finger in Li Po's bony chest,
nor can an orange be peeled without a fist fight.
Li Po takes another shot then falls backwards
off his tree stump. The mountain is hovering over him,
threatening to kick his ass. Li Po is not listening.
His thoughts have wandered toward the glow
of another indiscretion. Nobody will say it, but what everyone
wants to see is Li Po slap the mountain
in the face.

Recess

There, beneath the enormous
American Flag flapping so loud
we thought it was a crowd, we really
went to town. I mean we brutalized
the kid. *If you want your mommy*
to hold your hand, someone said (we had Ed
tied up now, rapping his knuckles
with a ruler while he squirmed), *then go back*
to Sunday school. It was awkward.
Everyone noticed my own hands
shaking, but something about this game
inspired me to try.

Sestina Aguilera

Christina Aguilera has a blue
tongue. That scream you hear when you drop her in
boiling water is actually just steam
escaping her shell. She invented the word
agnostic in 1869 because she was tired
of being called an atheist

by Baudelaire and Mallarmé.
To wit: she is the only platinum singer who, at room
temperature, acts as a liquid. The odds of her being injured
by a crowbar are somewhere around 13%, yet in
coal mines that percentage rises to a whopping 75. The word
Aguilera actually means *dreams*

with one eye open, while the word itself tastes like cream,
which tastes like beetles, which tastes
like apples, which tastes like worms,
which tastes like sleep deprived. You
cannot fold Christina Aguilera in half more than 7 times, yet in
Iceland it is against the law to keep her as a fire

arm. Ditto Siberia and in a Boeing 747. When her wires
kink and cannot be straightened by a team
of skeptics, this is called dog leg, which she sings beautifully of in
a number of her hit songs, including *Dirty*, *I Got Trouble*,
Slow Down Baby, *What a Girl Wants*, *The Way You
Talk To Me*, as well as in her cover version of *Word

To Your Mother* by Sir Vanillus Ice.
　　　Aguilera is the longest single syllable word
in English, and the only one that rotates on its side
and counterclockwise. As the youngest
Pope ever, (11 years old), she instituted one slot machine
per every eight citizens in Vegas.
Contrary to popular rumor, she keeps her heart in

her head like a shrimp or a pregnant goldfish. In
the Animal Crackers cookie zoo she appears
        as 15 different animal shapes, including a herd
of red blood cells, lighting bolts, and the Nobel Peace Prize.
It was said she trapped the wind like a tired
man. The HOPE radio station in Sweden continually beams
her lyrics into space. A bylaw in Utah

bans her from unionizing or having sex with a man in
        a moving ambulance. Or so it would seem on her
coat of arms, which reads: *In the beginning was the word...*
give me your tired, your poor, your huddled Aguileras yearning to be free.

in medias res

Herodotus gets bitch-slapped
on the banks of the Bosporus—
In the background Jimmy's Shrimp Shack
burns to the ground—
The dog days of summer
are thin letters & vice versa—
After dinner old man Ovid leans on the pisser
to keep from spilling over—
Everyone on the peninsula called him
Orville The Pigeon-Toed.
Is that my penis? Orville says.
It looks like a monk under house arrest—
Once the cuff
is wrapped around my arm
and she starts to pump
I'm all over Nurse Celeste—
I have an inoperable brain tumor
named Caesar—
I have Dante in the prison yard looking
Lady Dog in the eye—
Red lights on the jukebox
stutter like the hearts of pigeons on speed—
Time's pants pool at our ankles—
A shot rings out in the cathedral—
The Motel Secret Service comes knocking
because the music is too loud.
I answer the door nude
still wet from skinny-dipping
with exchange students—
Zeus lights a cigarette—
Careful boys, says the head of the Motel
Secret Service. *This guy used to be a teacher
in the Jersey public schools—*

Interview

-for Denise Duhamel

Where did you get your dehydrochlorinator?
From the unluckiness of the new left,
with my writ of mandamus
from the southern hemisphere.

Why did you decide to teach human rights?
Because they foster sentential calculus
with an axe to grind. Arterial inflammation
is all around us, speaking to our beavers
and distribution functions. This applies
to area codes as well.

What do on-ramps gain from area codes?
Specifically, fair market value
for cupcakes. A well-designed Bulgarian
home-girl is not strictly about funerals.
Area codes make stationary waves
with the ephemera. The modus vivendi
of guillotines for example, or clay pigeons
in chicken-fried steak. Such stud poker says
sonatas about what peppered-moths can achieve.

Is it important to onside kick?
Knowing how certainly broadens our thongs
and encourages refried beans. Franklin Stoves,
why teddy bears coincide with nausea,
how some attorneys regard epiblasts; to practice
this croquet develops not just our perspiration
but also our inner pervert.

And the majorette polar bear when you clean and jerk?
Actually, I have a little extemporization.
I just hope stumped-tailed macaques understand
that hubble-bubble, whetstone, whey-face,

wheat bread and by whoopee cushion
reveal son et lumière about the culvert.

So you agree then with area codes?
Accidentally.

Do you think stumped-tailed macaques actually
absorb the infundibulum?
Somnambulists do. Thrashers who ignore
ingrates reveal more about theogony
than the sublime, especially with clavichords.
In estate agents, human rights
is the stumblebum of being. Area codes too.
It's not a matzo ball that interests
evening stars, but no alternative medicine
should strike them from our stones.

Footnotes to the Poem "Matt's Rhodendrum of Shame"

-annotations by Josh Bell

1

2

3

4

5

6

7

8

9

10

11

12

---

1. *Trigger....trigger*: veiled reference to Hamlet's "to be or not to be" soliloquy.
2. In the late 20th century, the stomach of the totemic magnum platypus was lined with cranberries, then ingested by a shaman. Here, the poet imagines the stomach lined with Platonic philosophy, and therefore envisions such classical thought as ground down to service idiosyncratic modern tradition. Plato's Stones was also the name of Guenette's failed musical group of the 1970s, whose one album was entitled *Punk Rock Girls of Antiquity*.
3. Rhetorical.
4. Guenette had this claim tested at UCLA's sophisticated poetry laboratories, where the poem "Howl" underwent grueling study. Though results were inconclusive regarding its literary merits, "Howl" was found to be 25 percent less absorbent than other poems written that same year.
5. *What...fling*: In an interview in APR, Guenette later disowned this line, claiming that leprechauns wrote it.
   ie, diaries.
6. Reference to the image of infinity as a snake eating its own tail. Also, the phallus.
7. Allusion to Yeats' famous line, as many critics have imagined, but also an echo of a popular television commercial for a paper towel rumored to be 25 percent more absorbent than competitors, and therefore a reference back to Ginsberg.
8. The entire poem turns on itself in this manner, much like the disillusioned snake, above.
9. *Porn Star*: Guenette himself. Also, Jesus.
10. *lonely...maker*: this vision of the godhead betrays the poet's interest in Gnostic mysticism.

13

14

15

16

17

18

19

20

21

22

23

24

25

---

11. *"the colonel"* is clearly Sigmund Freud. The mashed potatoes are too beautiful to look at.

12. No...first: Harsh words directed at Guenette's godfather, TS Eliot.

13. At one point this footnote read "made you look, you dirty crook," but the editors feared it would further alienate the reader. Now this footnote simply reads: "Matt's Rhododendron of Shame is a hardy shrub growing in the North American mountains of the Appalachian chain."

14. Rhetorical. Also, we were our own control group.

15. Re: this line, and the following, lawsuits are pending.

16. ie, through the poems of yore, in which we were both the gardener and the gardened.

17. Apparently a famous race-car driver.

18. A curious construction, wherein Love's Hammer is envisioned as having hands with which it grips, when everyone knows that Love's Hammer keeps its hands free, so that we might kneel and lick them.

19. Freud again.

20 Rhetorical. Note to Matt: How about a line where you use the word "spavined"?

21 The man who is a woman is Tiresias, the blind seer. The poet visualizes himself as humping the personification of wisdom, a typical conceit of this time period.

22. If memory serves, Tiresias was from Thebes, not Milwaukee.

23. Again, an inanimate object imagined as having hands with which it might hug or grip, when everyone knows the haiku keeps its hands free, so that we might kneel and lick them.

24. ie, Folsom. The poet is actually writing this in prison.

25. He's quibbling here.

26

27

28

29

30

31

---

26. Guenette was, in fact, a member of the Green Party, and wrote several manifestos on recycling.
27. Rhetorical.
28. *When...fog*: In an earlier draft, this passage read: "When I open my eyes, I better not see that miserable ferret again," but his editor struck it, and provided these present lines without his knowledge. It was published with her changes, though Guenette never knew it. He continued to read it in its original form when touring. Until his death, he referred to it as "the ferret poem," and when interviewer Charlie Rose quoted it to him with the lines his editor had provided, Guenette tore off his shirt and issued a challenge to all comers. A cue-card girl testified that Guenette wept as he then, as if in apology, invited Rose back to his home to watch the 70s exploitation film *Cockfighter*.
29. In the original folio, this line read "Sometimes I hear/elevator music, smell lemmings," but this is an obvious error. I have replaced "lemmings" with "lemons," but a good case has been made for both "lemurs" and "Germans."
30 *Rojelio and The Bear* was a popular children's book; Rojelio was also the nickname of Guenette's cellmate at Folsom, one Johnny Roger Walker, former investment banker, who, in Guenette's will, inherited a bus pass and a packet of hairnets.
31. In other words, "I am worse in forgiving my own sins than I even was in sinning." A side note: The reference to "15 minutes" is rather interesting, because Guenette, famously, could not tell time.

Sonnet

We've reached the part of the freak show
where the freaks in their six
degrees of separation have been exposed
although with much indecision.

It's time now for "An die Freude"
from the fourth part of Beethoven's Ninth
as suddenly one freak gets a hasty
senseless crack in the nuts

from another in a crowded Italian piazza
as all around scores of pigeons
take flight, some of them shitting

all within sight of The Bishop
whose kisses are for humankind
but whose help seems to never arrive.

Poem

Sometimes I'd drive
to the airport
just to wander the terminals,
an insomniac wannabe Whitman
in a casino of blown leaves,

would watch the old Greek woman
in her upside down
pineapple dress sell a Zen garden
of trinkets to new arrivals,

the hungry couples
kissing at the gates like protesters
doused in kerosene, their tongues
the blue hiss of a match.

I eavesdropped on suits
named Don and The Colonel
as they prattled
into cell phones moving
some Africa of information
like a hive of killer bees.

A religious experience
late-night variety show
starring cannibals, The Psychedelic
Furs, and Philip K. Dick.

It healed me so good
I thought everyone was Jesus.

Silver Spoons: The Lost Episodes

Boys Will Be Boys: Ricky and Alfonso double-team an underage girl who may or may not be related to Alfonso. Later, after blowing up a warehouse with a hijacked fuel tanker, the boys go on the lam to Chicago with Federal Agents in hot pursuit. Mr. T guest stars.

The Best Christmas Ever: Ricky wanders through a dream, tending after two mysterious dogs and cleaning up his dead mother's trashed house. Lots of crying. Erin Gray guest stars as a kindhearted U.S. Postal worker.

Spare the Rod: Ricky, suddenly a college professor, confronts an angry mob of students who are resentful of his seemingly inconsistent and contradictory pedagogy. Milton Berle's legendary genitalia stars as the standardized test that meddles with Ricky's curriculum development one time too many.

What's Cookin'?: In this 33-second episode, guest-directed by a guy randomly chosen from a Milwaukee street corner, Ricky, in a room filling up with sunlight, contemplates the sublime and then immediately feels stupid.

Judgment Day: Alfonso "comes out," learns Norwegian, gets a job in a nursing home, and teaches Dexter the Nursing Home Sponge Bath Mantra: "Labia majora, Labia minora, mons in the back, mons in the back." Ricky and his millionaire father go bowling. Edward Stratton III rolls a perfect game on Vicodin.

Popular Children's Games: A Pre-20th Century Count Up

Sinner
Funeral
Child Bride
Dover Beach
Reconstruction
Arena Football
Truth or Stoning
Outhouse Scurvy Judge
Ring around the Leper
Burn the Church Records
Feral Cat Apostate Hater
Smear the Queer with Rickets
Pin the Tail on the Immigrant
Pre-Pubescent Woolen Mill Worker

Solid Mineral Matter, A Felted Sheet of Fibers, Cutting Instrument
of Two Blades Whose Cutting Edges
Slide Past Each Other

Future Poem

The tournament brackets of our fate
decorate the cafeteria plates, chairs liquefy down
like tears from above,
and there's shitloads of gluey blue stuff everywhere.

Life hints of an ordered docility,
a soupy lucidity,
a saturated toxicity.

You can hear it in the oxidized buzz
of overgrown wasps, taste it in the super-strong
pina-coladas they serve outside church.

Lifetimes can vaporize like luck in the nitrogen-fueled
effluvium, and among the swank aliens,
whose glabrous skin
shimmers like locks, bean-thin is in, the better-mannered
speaking like Shakespearean bards.

As in the days of yore,
if you can levitate iron shavings off a mirrored
marble slab, hostesses will summon forth
hermaphroditic slaves with wine.

Surprisingly the El Camino is back, tricked out
with an hourglass cockpit and thermal-guided
personnel annihilators.

That's the good news.

The bad is our anxiety and fear,
stretched through nine dimensions
like an interstellar limo.

As children we'll assemble robots
in exchange for our absent fathers; they'll guard
our delicate bodies
as the cosmos speeds us through.

When the robots grow lonely
with dents and stuttered gears,

when you find them in the swiveling hover-cafes
sipping oily tea, reading a poetry
of zeros and ones,

you'll look into their honeycombed, pink-lit eyes,
and know exactly what they think.

Kosmikophobia

-after Hegel

That which is in itself can be called *dildo*, and that what is for another—what is known as knowledge—can be called *penetration*. But being-for-another is also called *dildo*—in the sense of that which it stands against—and accordingly, what the dildo is in and of itself is called its *bliss* or its *penetration*. In both instances, if we can be just a little bit open and curious to experiment, we can hope to experience whether and how the *dildo* corresponds to its *penetration*, and how the *penetration* corresponds, *blissfully*, to its *dildo*.

In Case

We popped rhinoceros pills
like it was a varsity sport.
They charged us into bone-filled clouds,
helped us gore one thing at a time.
Once it was dusk, your body shaking,
helicopters hovering everywhere.
I made a prediction:
next time we fell in love
it would be with a slowness, but not so slow
we'd slip irretrievably into comas.
We felt the planet chased through space.
You called it a blessing.
I said a weapon.

Exquisite Platypus

The platypus's exotic features and stout build
make egg-laying a breeze. Jimmy, let's review the tape. Here
we see Nicolette, a platypus from the outback, throwing
up so much kibble even experts
don't know what to do. Rocky was watching
this on TV. He found the peanut brittle and Gideon Bible
in the nightstand. It was so like him not to know
where he was, and Rocky was like nobody else. That's why
they voted him Duke of the Condo Association
just before they quartered his hens. Oh yes, Rocky said.
It was coming back to him now...

Summer Slideshow

Here's where I backed the get-away car
into a mailbox three years wide.

*

Here's where I pepper-sprayed the neighbor's
doorknobs, carved a boat from the barbed trees
of my intentions, filled it up with jagged
rocks for friends.

*

A drag-queen named Buddy Holly worked the river bars
his sequined gown a disposable
skin that drove drunks crazy
in the American night.
(say cheese!)

*

I worked the synthetics factory's graveyard shift
where it was 1832
and my attitude
an eleven-year-old boy
with vertigo and tuberculosis.

*

Packed plastic cups like the ones I pissed in
for a boss once a month.

*

(Scene deleted)

*

The destinations were
lonely planets—
Davenport, Des Moines, Waterloo—

busy tones for
the wrong numbers
I dialed again and again.

*

In those days if some asshole planted a burning cross
in your lawn
cops would write it off
as a gardening tip.

*

At the adult video store the cashier wore a turban
preserving the date palms
of his thoughts.

*

A slaughter-house filled downtown with the sugared
stink of processed ham.

*

One night the manager nudged me open
like a suitcase; out spilled nothing but mismatched socks.

*

We eyed a conveyor belt clogged with duct tape
and glue.

*

What do you make of it?
he said, a match of blame rising to strike in his voice.

*

Almost like that I was saved.

If You're Lucky Decent Jobs Turn Up in the Paper

One day you're in bed
with the dancing queen
you think you love,

the next you're watching pigeons
flounce around a fountain
and nothing is ever the same,

agony of fast food, agony of suitcases,
agony of West Virginia
after funnel clouds and rain.

The drawbridge draws up,
in the distance
rows of orange cones,

a boisterous wind, a Chihuahua
pissing in the azaleas,
his amazing Chihuahua testicles

squinty acorns in the sun.
Wise up, the traffic shouts,
honking a horn for every bruised

and wobbly heart.
The heart wallpapered, the heart harbored
like a mistress, shaped like a hoof.

Even the shrubs
will speak in harsh whispers,
making shrubby jokes

about your savings account
and lumpy futon couch.
You will find yourself scratching lottery tickets

like a rash. You will dream of Finland,
you will strangle your friends
with stupid questions like *What kind of sub shop*

closes before five? Who invented the tube top?
Pegasus of the gas pumps,
Madonna of the information booth,

guitarist rocking the church steps
in a paroxysm of rapture/delirium/grief.
Don't worry, says the stranger

to his shoes, *the Jersey quarters are being
minted as we speak.*
Any day now the experts will announce

Gilligan's Island was an allegory
for string theory.
Rounds of beer will mysteriously appear.

Light in photo yellows at its edge.
It will remind you of a mouth
stuffed with flowers, a lover

naked and adding garlic to the sauce.

Metamorphoses

-after Adrian Matejka's *Devil's Garden*

1. Caesura

heat lightning
sliced the night
kung-fu style

i leaned
into the tornado siren's
racket-blast solo

saw your skirt
a hula-hoop
of flames

in the just-then rain

2. Here Nor There

students from the party
struck matches
beneath our window

flames hissed to

snuffed themselves out
like stars
like chest pains

all day my heart swims

a fish through ash
through the memory
of itself

all night ghost cars

rev engines
gun the intersections
of my dreams

next morning

you found them
bottle caps on the steps
arranged to spell

we   are   here

3. Definite

red mood records
radio-spun

you gave
the swirl-and-sway

water soaking my socks
like a dare

here you said
slipped down the hall

desire filled
by the smoke
of your absence

morning
rain-flamed
glitter-streets

heard
the trap door's tic

a sadness
rising from the yard

you stripped
from your dress

a certainty
emerging from a dream

watched you feed
that dress to the trees

Misconduct

We slow-zoomed in
thumbed the violations

of our desires
like detectives on vacation

your undercover skirt hiked up
my Devil's Garden beach shirt undone.

We vodka jello-ed & stilettoed
a peep-hole in the cosmos

flipped like a pancake
& slipped it in our files for luck.

Your tongue's hipbone
hooked my ear, rush-delivered

my heart's stomach, cha-chinged
my dirty thoughts like lotto tickets.

Swallowed like a smuggler
swallows wire, I felt you rise through me

the sun-burnt moon
through the day's pink throat.

The city hung a hundred signs
around its neck: pool-hall

for the double-crossed, martinis
for dizzy-assed pranksters. You said

let's disguise ourselves as trench coats
and erase each other's halos.

Our marriage a disorderly conduct
like high heels down an alley

Pistols at the center
of our own conspiracy.

Suddenly one long fuse.

Vow

We wallpapered the Three-Legged Sack Pantry
with sticky notes. We stuck sticky notes inside
The Broken Ham Pie Warmer, and on the Ceiling
Vibrators in the Den of Fake Happenings.
We recorded everything-our China Syndromes
and Sarasota Backslaps, our Just Enoughs
and Peachy Greens. We turned our sublet
into a Reflection Seeking Yellow Trail.
When we got bored with the What Was we started
making lists. Our first one was called Four
Four Word Sentences You Never Want to Hear.
The first three sentences were easy enough-
1)   This ain't no DEE-troit.
2)   Put on some Skynard!
3)   Start the Syntactical Analysis
-but the fourth sentence eluded us
like The Celestial Swan. Then one night my lover
had me tied to a post in The Big Curtain Fortress Garden.
She was interrogating me with the wooden spoons
according to The Pamphlet Of Punishment
with Various Oils: Peanut, Olive, and Motor.
Whatever you're doing back there, I said, I love it.
Pain gunned through my body like Exquisite
Architecture. The last thing I heard before
I blacked out was my lover saying, that's NOT my finger...
Thus as luck would have it we completed our list.

The Today Show

My daydream where Katie Couric wanders
through the rubble. Her beige pant suit torn
and covered with filth. Her eyes gone wild
she lets loose her primal scream, radiates
fear, twitches and growls as I draw near.

Yet I coax Katie into my arms,
wrap her in a blanket, take her home.
If I could, if I could save Katie
Couric, help her heal, the effort would bring
my family, the lost city, together.

We would keep a constant vigil, play smooth
jazz, administer proton beam therapy
in the church basement. Later soldiers
would come by to see what we were doing.
They'd take one look at Katie, the raw skin
suffering her arms and legs, the protective
lamp shade around her head, and say
we should put her out of her misery.

But she would be family then,
a citizen, her pain having made the war
real in a way TV never could.
I would tell the soldiers to look into
her eyes, and see that Katie Couric had
the will and right to live.

:Ode Version

Love, your jukebox with iridescent
sequins, light stippled reflections
like silver bruises. I should know better
from good-bye, lingering like a bowl
of bar nuts. Had I more than an expired
bus pass in my pocket, I could catch
a ride on Johnny Cash's voice,
its back-in-black *basso profundo*,
through the late hours all the way
to Memphis

to say I'm sorry, to say I've learned
nothing from our irreducible scenes:
me standing there in the wet street yellow-
dusted with pollen, you driving away
not towards transcendence, just another
city, in a struggling shit-box
that never looked back. I came here
on a hunch, to these flowerings furious
and distracted, to sit among
the minor gospels of cigarettes
and emptying bottles, to hear
the thundercrack of a cue driving home
the eight.

It reminds me of hunger, wires swallowed
by kudzu, the two of us showered
in neon and the city pushed forward
like a drink. I remember your fingers
stroking the inside of my wrist.
Surely as the past sheds light for new light,
as our bodies once blossomed like ashes
our breath resisted every word.

Arkhein

Dreaming of X again.
That time she said, *What goes better*
with the tumor, the red felt hat or the green?
From a dream the highway flowers
with shadows.
Hermes the shoplifter's shopping cart,
god obsidian, inexorable,
and at the corner of the corn field
the still burned-out church.
Dreaming is history.
A certain lake where fear is struck
into the hearts of bluegill all summer long.
The summer I committed suicide
a thousand times throwing myself beneath
Indiana's dumb tires.
I remember the heart-gun with its
serial numbers filed clean, but the brain
was an abandoned strip mall.
We know the dream is other dreams smashed
to fragments but sometimes the fragments
fight back.
Starlight disassembles from the stars.
They look palm-sized and edible
from the highway.
I have to be careful then not to step
from myself and get snagged like something
in the trees.
Dreaming of X a white flame
in purple surf.
The dream where I can say I was met
with love.

The Town

I stuck my hand
through the window jagged with glass
dad said not to screw with
now this scar worms over my wrist.
Some punks John knows row out to the island

to jerk off and play with matches.
In the rain Steve books it from the cops
slips and screams, the bone seaming from his wrist
while the rest of us are still in the field
launching bottle rockets at cars.

Later when the island is going up in flames
it's the most exciting thing to happen
in years. The town comes down
to the shore cracking beers
and cranking up AC/DC. The fire funnels

brilliantly toward its terrible god.
The punks John knows secretly row back
that fall we take turns
tip-toeing outside Chrissie's bedroom
where Chrissie and her sister are in t-shirts

and panties playing with chinchillas.
Who will speak for this? the town says
in a language everyone's heard
but hardly anyone listens anymore.
As the island went up in flames

I worried would the fish boil in the weeds.
Steve's mother showed up with a just-hit dog
in the trunk and some words for whoever
was running the circus. Fire trucks circled
like idiots in the pit on the far shore.

Later I'm behind the roller rink with Steve.
Some punks John knows are about
to sell us some weed.   Who will apologize for you?
the town says. Who shall be thanked
for all that's been done?

Sudden Anthem

It was snowing so hard
I thought we were inside the stretched out
belly of an arctic pig. I was afraid
if I ventured through the storm
I'd be erased halfway to the swings.
It was the Age of Aquarius. I had starmaps

for eyes, thoughts like rats
down an alley of dumpsters.
This was back in kindergarten.
I carried a Star Wars lunchbox,
and an attitude like Jupiter.
I wore Spiderman UnderRoos.
I still peed the bed after scary dreams

but knew where to fence the sheets.
The other kids were gone.
They'd disappeared like postage stamps,
licked away clean on their mothers' tongues.
I was the sole candlepin
wobbling at a small round table,
a single lamp

shining down, inventing me like hope
as I practiced writing my name.
See me through the shook up
snow globe of memory, eager and serious
like a lawyer with his mistress,
like a muscle car ramped on skids. See me

chewing my lips like I do now,
whenever I take hammer to nails,
a 40-pound shoulder hunched over
like a question,

an astronaut planting the flag of his pencil
in the yellow moonscape
of a page.

Acknowledgments

Many thanks to the following journals where some of these poems first appeared:

Best American Grocery Lists 2006: "Milk, Milk, Lemonade"
Field & Stream: "Vince Neil's Marathon Training Schedule"
C=R=A=P Q=U=A=R=T=E=R=L=Y: "? Industrial + -Industrial = --Ind[US]Trial"
The Hoboken Review: "Get Your Greasy Hands Off My Porsche, Walt Whitman" and "Poem Coming Out of My Ears"
Slate: "Ferrous Reduction Spheres"
McSweeney's Rejects: "Sestina Aguilera"
Melancholy Bastard: The Journal of Finnish American Arts & Letters: "Sisu and Pulla"
Lawn & Landscape Magazine: "The American Lawn"
The Akron Beacon Nordic Journal of Linguistic Dysfunction:: "Akron Darklings"
The Vatican City Review: "Songs of Abstinence"
Poet Whore: "The Terrible Beautiful Things I Wrote About Gravity in Workshop"
SEIZURE! The Epileptic Lesbian with Tourette's Review: A Journal by Epileptic Lesbians with Tourette's for Epileptic Lesbians with Tourette's: "A Ghazal for Muncie, Indiana"
Etcetera, Etcetera: "..."

Acknowledgments

Grateful acknowledgement is given to the following journals where these poems, sometimes in slightly different versions, first appeared:

Another Chicago Magazine: "A Brief History of the Home Gym"
Diagram: "Etymology" (originally published as "Nickname Letter"), "The Town" and "Li Po Poem"
The Greensboro Review: "Metamorphoses"
Mannequin Envy: "Sestina Aguilera"
Melic Review: "Interview"
Passages North: "The Happening"
Poetry Midwest: "Exquisite Platypus"and "Silver Spoons: the Lost Episodes"
Sojourn: "Fracture Poem" (originally published as "Compound Fractures")
Southern Indiana Review: "Vow," and "Vortex: The Super-Sized Supermarket"

The following poems appeared in the chapbook *Hush of Something Endless* (Ropewalk Press, 2006): "Hush of Something Endless," "Secret Life of the Coin-Operated Laundromat Owner," "Homeric," "Recess," "Poem," "Other Items from Occam's Bathroom," "Future Poem" (originally published in *Diagram*), "In Case" "If You're Lucky Decent Jobs Turn Up in the Paper" (originally published in *Quarterly West*), and "Sudden Anthem"

Special thanks to Brett Ralph, Sophia Kartsonis, Dawn Tefft, Steve Long, Steve Forrester, David Dodd Lee, Kathryn Kerr, Jim McGarrah, and Paul Guest.

For everyone at SIU, especially my amazing teachers: Allison Joseph, Rodney Jones and Lucia Perillo.

For my what if? brothers: Josh Bell, Mike Theune, and Ron Mitchell. I'd be lost without you.

For my wife Julie and my family (I love you), and especially for my mother, Karen Emily (Pasanen) Schneider: we miss you.

Matthew Guenette grew up in the Connecticut River Valley in Newport, New Hampshire. He received a BA in English from the University of New Hampshire, and an MFA from Southern Illinois University. He has worked as a busboy, landscaper, and salesclerk. He lives with his wife Julie in Madison, WI, and teaches at Madison Area Technical College.

Printed in the United States
125507LV00006B/94-120/P